Sea Horses & Pipefish

Contents

Text by Stanley L. Swartz
Photography by Robert Yin

DOMINIE PRESS
Pearson Learning Group

About Sea Horses

The sea horse is a **strange** fish.

Its head looks like a horse's head.

Its tail looks like a monkey's tail.

◀ Brown Sea Horse

Sea horses use their tails to hold on to things. Their bodies are covered by bony **armor**. This armor **protects** them.

◀ Yellow Sea Horse

How Sea Horses Swim

Sea horses swim with their heads up and their tails down. They **bob** up and down in the water. When they move up and down they look like the horses on a **carousel**.

◀ Yellow Sea Horse

How Sea Horses Are Born

Baby sea horses are born in an unusual way. The mother sea horse lays eggs in a **pouch** on the father's belly. The father carries the eggs until they **hatch**.

◀ Sea Horse in Algae

How Sea Horses Hide

This sea horse looks like a **dragon**.
It easily blends in with the seaweed.
It hides and waits for its dinner
to drift by.

◀ Leafy Dragon Sea Horse

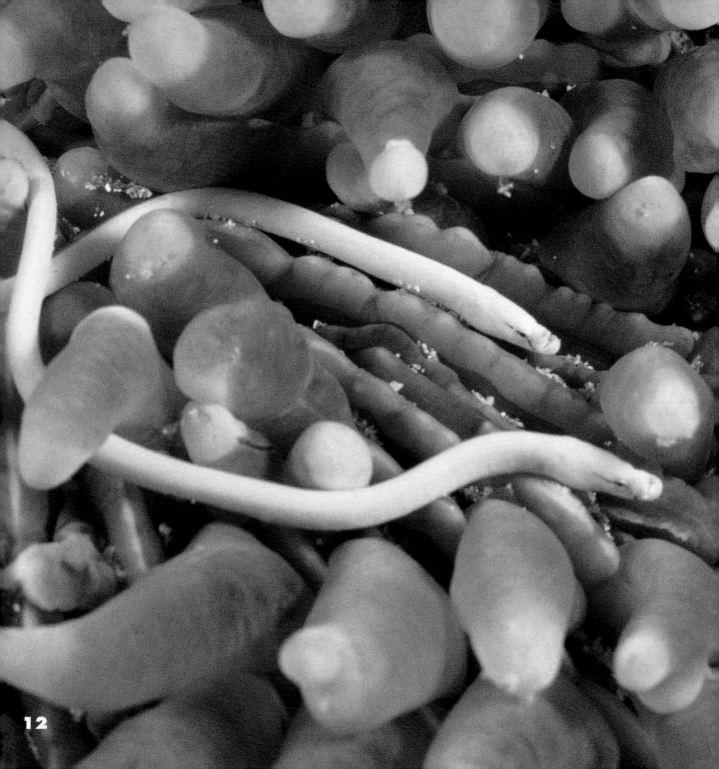

About Pipefish

The pipefish is a **cousin** of the
sea horse. It has a thin body.
Some pipefish look like worms.

◀ Pipefish on Mushroom Coral

Pipefish are not very big. They can be up to six inches long. This **diver** has a good view of this pipefish.

◀ **Diver with Ghost Pipefish**

The Banded Pipefish

The banded pipefish has a spot
on its tail that looks like a head.
Its long, narrow **snout** looks like
a tail.

◀ Banded Pipefish

Underwater Beauties

Sea horses and pipefish can be very **colorful**. Colors help to protect them in case of danger. Some sea horses and pipefish can even change colors.

◀ Ghost Pipefish

Sea horses and pipefish live mostly in warm, shallow waters. Their eyes move **independently** of each other. This means they can look in two directions at once.

◄ Ghost Pipefish on Gray Coral

This pipefish blends in with the **background**. This makes it very hard to see. Sea horses and pipefish are very **exotic** sea animals.

◀ **Pipefish**

Glossary

armor:	A tough, protective covering
background:	Close surroundings
bob:	To move up and down
carousel:	A moving platform; a merry-go-round
colorful:	Having many bright colors
cousin:	A close relative
diver:	Someone who goes under water to study marine life
dragon:	A make-believe monster
exotic:	Strange; unusual
hatch:	To break out of an egg
independently:	Separately
pouch:	An opening that looks like a bag or a sack
protect:	To keep from being harmed or injured
snout:	A long nose
strange:	Different or unusual

Index